钱的故事

How We Organize Ourselves | Non-Fiction Series

Copyright © 2022 by Level Learning, INC. and Washington Yu Ying PCS™
Original and Edited Text Copyright © 2022 by Washington Yu Ying PCS™

All rights reserved. No part of this book in whole or part may be reproduced without written permission from the publisher.

Published by Level Learning, INC.

Content Contributors:
Washington Yu Ying PCS™ - Shuo Li, Pearl Zao He You
Level Learning - Jingyao Qi

Illustrations by: Matt Austin

Leveling classification based on Level Learning standard.
For full description, visit www.levellearning.com

ISBN 978-1-64040-117-4
Simplified Chinese Edition

About Level Learning:

Level Learning provides a literacy focused curriculum specifically designed for K-12 Chinese as a Second Language classrooms. Our program offers 20 levels of specific and detailed objectives, leveled texts and passages, mastery-based online assessment, and analytics to enable data-driven instruction. Level Learning reading curriculum for both literature and informational text emphasize grammar and comprehension skills to help teachers develop confident and independent Chinese language readers. The non-fiction series of books are specifically designed to support our informational text course based on multiple national standards. To learn more about our entire offering, visit www.levellearning.com.

About Washington Yu Ying PCS™:

Washington Yu Ying PCS is a Mandarin English dual language immersion International Baccalaureate (IB) World school. Yu Ying's mission is to inspire and prepare young people to create a better world by challenging them to reach their full potential in a nurturing Chinese/English educational environment. Yu Ying's comprehensive IB, dual immersion curriculum equips students with global competencies for success in the real world. As a leader in immersion education, Yu Ying is determined to advance Chinese language programs and global citizenry education by helping other schools create and strengthen their Chinese programs. For more information, email: products@washingtonyuying.org

很久很久以前，世界上还没有钱，人们如果需要一件物品，会拿自己的东西和别人交换。

怎么交换呢？交换物品的价值应该差不多。比如，我用一头小猪交换你的一只小羊。

大约公元前1200年,人们开始用贝壳来换取自己想要的东西。比如说,五个贝壳可以买一头小猪。贝壳是最早的货币。

那时候世界上每个地方用的货币都不一样。有的地方用贝壳,有的地方用漂亮的石头,有的地方用小鸟的羽毛等。

大约在公元前1000年，中国人开始使用金属货币。金属货币是用什么做的呢？有的金属货币是用铜做的，有的是用金做的，还有的是用银做的。

可是,有时候拿太多的金属货币不方便。于是聪明的人们又发明了银票。银票很轻,使用起来非常方便。

现在,人们使用纸币和硬币,但越来越多的人也开始使用其它的支付方法,比如信用卡、手机支付等。人们的生活真是越来越方便了!

Glossary

	Pinyin	English Definition
世界	shì jiè	world
钱	qián	money
如果	rú guǒ	if
物品	wù pǐn	goods
交换	jiāo huàn	to trade, to exchange
价值	jià zhí	value
大约	dà yuē	about, approximately
公元前	gōng yuán qián	BC, BCE
贝壳	bèi ké	shell
买	mǎi	to buy
货币	huò bì	currency
羽毛	yǔ máo	feather
硬币	yìng bì	coin
铜	tóng	copper

	Pinyin	English Definition
金	jīn	gold
银	yín	silver
方便	fāng biàn	convenient
发明	fā míng	to invent
纸币	zhǐ bì	paper bill
越来越	yuè lái yuè	more and more
支付	zhī fù	to pay
方法	fāng fǎ	method
信用卡	xìn yòng kǎ	credit card
手机	shǒu jī	cell phone, mobile phone
金属	jīn shǔ	metal
银票	yín piào	banknote with a value in silver in ancient times

www.ingramcontent.com/pod-product-compliance
Lightning Source LLC
Chambersburg PA
CBHW041226070526
44584CB00001B/119